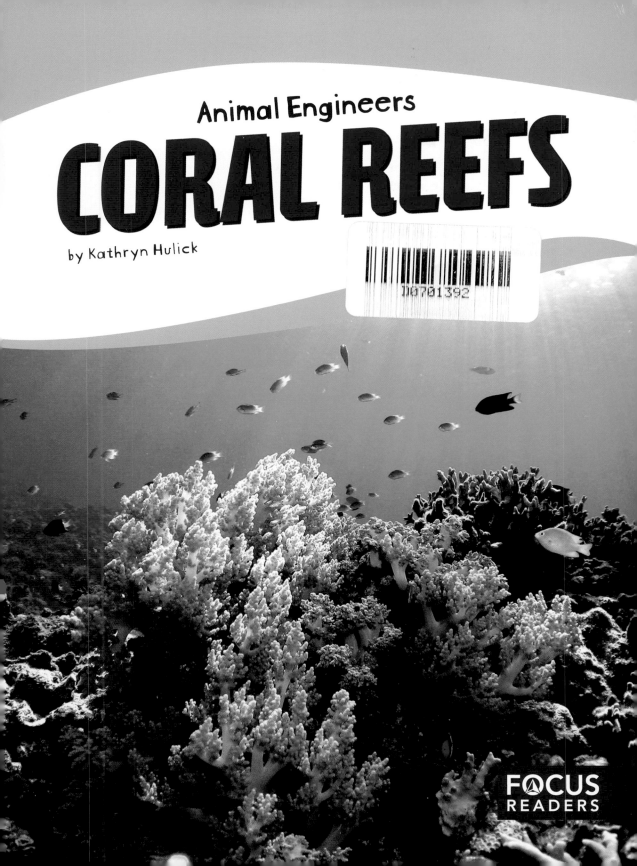

Animal Engineers
CORAL REEFS

by Kathryn Hulick

FOCUS READERS

FOCUS READERS

www.focusreaders.com

Focus Readers is distributed by North Star Editions:
sales@northstareditions.com | 888-417-0195

Produced for Focus Readers by Red Line Editorial.

Photographs ©: Masahiro Suzuki/Shutterstock Images, cover, 1; johnandersonphoto/iStockphoto, 4–5; aquapix/Shutterstock Images, 7, 16–17; Ethan Daniels/Shutterstock Images, 8–9, 14–15; Ruslan Mamedov/Shutterstock Images, 11; tororo reaction/Shutterstock Images, 13; Borisoff/Shutterstock Images, 19; Ekkapan Poddamrong/Shutterstock Images, 21; Isabelle Kuehn/Shutterstock Images, 22–23; Laura Dinraths/Shutterstock Images, 25, 29; Dudarev Mikhail/Shutterstock Images, 27

ISBN
978-1-63517-861-6 (hardcover)
978-1-63517-962-0 (paperback)
978-1-64185-165-7 (ebook pdf)
978-1-64185-064-3 (hosted ebook)

Library of Congress Control Number: 2018931112

Printed in the United States of America
Mankato, MN
May, 2018

About the Author

Kathryn Hulick has been writing for children for 10 years. Her books include *Awesome Science: Dinosaurs* and *Robot Innovations: Medical Robots*. She also writes articles for *Muse* magazine and the Science News for Students website. On her honeymoon, she went snorkeling among the coral reefs of the Caribbean. This book is dedicated to her son, who loves watching fish.

TABLE OF CONTENTS

CHAPTER 1

PALACES UNDER THE SEA

An orange fish darts in and out of tunnels. Rocky towers reach up around them. Below them are walls and caves. Together, these shapes look like an underwater palace. But this palace is a coral **reef**.

 **Coral reefs look like rock. But they are alive.**

Reefs are made by tiny animals called corals. Most corals live in **colonies**. Each colony is made up of thousands of coral **polyps**. Polyps have soft bodies. But they make hard shells. The shells protect the polyps. When many corals join together, a reef forms.

FUN FACT

Coral polyps are tiny. Most are small enough to fit on the tip of a pencil.

▷ **Many coral polyps join together to form a colony.**

There are many **species** of corals. Only some build reefs. Soft corals do not build reefs. These corals look like plants. Corals that build reefs are called stony corals.

CHAPTER 2

HOW A REEF FORMS

A reef begins with just one coral polyp. The polyp attaches to a rock or the sea floor. Then it forms a hard cup around itself. The cup is made from the same material as a clam shell.

Coral reefs often form in shallow water near the coast.

Next, the polyp divides. A new polyp is formed. This new polyp attaches to the first one's shell. It forms its own cup. The polyps keep dividing. They build many cups on top of one another. Over time, they form a colony. Multiple colonies join together to form a reef.

FUN FACT

One type of coral is shaped like a brain.

Brain coral can grow up to 6 feet (1.8 m) tall.

Many coral species build reefs. They make a wide variety of shapes. Some form long branches. Others make flat platforms. Some corals even look like round domes.

The coral's shape also depends on the **habitat**. In places with big waves, corals tend to be strong and flat. In calmer areas, corals may be thinner or more delicate.

Some corals grow less than 1 inch (2.5 cm) each year. Others,

FUN FACT

The Great Barrier Reef in Australia is the biggest reef in the world. It is so big that astronauts can see it from outer space.

The Great Barrier Reef is more than 1,400 miles (2,250 km) long.

such as staghorn coral, can add up

to 8 inches (20 cm) every year.

REEF SHAPES

There are several kinds of coral reefs. Fringing reefs are most common. They grow close to coasts. Barrier reefs grow farther away from the coast. A lagoon separates them from shore. Sometimes an island with a fringing reef sinks under the sea. But the reef continues to grow. It becomes an **atoll**. This kind of reef is shaped like a circle.

Coral reefs can be very large. But they take a long time to form. A reef can take 10,000 years to form. Barrier reefs and atolls are often even older. They can take more than 100,000 years to form.

A fringing reef surrounds this island in the Banda Sea.

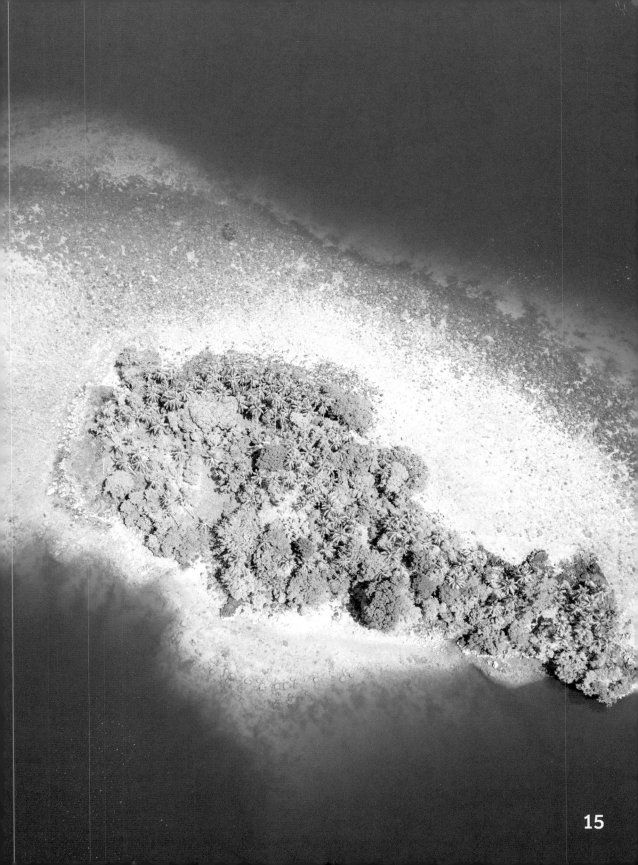

CHAPTER 3

AMAZING ALGAE

Coral polyps stay hidden inside their shells during the day. At night, they reach their tentacles out into the water. These soft arms are around the polyp's mouth. They can sting and catch food.

> **These stony coral polyps have their tentacles extended.**

Corals also get energy from **algae**. The algae live inside the polyps. Algae take in sunlight. They turn it into food. The algae keep some of this food. But they share some of it with the corals. Corals use energy from the food to make their shells. In return, the corals protect the algae.

FUN FACT

Most corals stay stuck in the same place their whole lives.

 Algae can make corals look green, brown, red, and orange.

Coral polyps are see-through. But algae are colorful. Their colors show through the clear corals. They give the reef its color.

Algae need sunlight. For this reason, corals tend to live in clear, shallow water. Most reefs are less than 230 feet (70 m) below the surface.

Algae also need warm water. Corals grow well in water that is between 70 and 85 degrees Fahrenheit (21 and 29°C).

But Earth's oceans are getting warmer. When the water is too hot, the algae leave the polyps. This can kill the corals.

> When algae leave, the corals turn white. This process is known as bleaching.

Water may also become more **acidic**. The acid eats away at the polyps' shells. It weakens the reef. Parts of the reef may break down and die.

CHAPTER 4

A COLORFUL COMMUNITY

Coral reefs are home to many kinds of ocean life. Some plants and animals even help build the reef. For instance, seaweed grows on reefs. When the seaweed dies, its **remains** form part of the reef.

Sea turtles eat the seaweed that grows on coral reefs.

Algae can help form reefs as well. Clams, oysters, and sponges also attach to reefs. Coral polyps build on top of them.

Seahorses, sea anemones, and starfish live on coral reefs. The crown-of-thorns starfish even eats coral. This starfish has many spines.

FUN FACT

Parrotfish chomp on the hard coral. Their bellies grind it up.

A colorful parrotfish swims near a coral reef.

Large and small fish swim near reefs. Many fish have bright colors and patterns. This helps them hide in the colorful corals. The corals protect the fish from **predators**. Some fish eat the corals, too.

Coral reefs also help protect the coast. The reefs act like a barrier. Waves must go past the reefs to reach the shore. In this way, the reefs help prevent **erosion**.

It is important to protect coral reefs. Many plants and animals depend on them for food and

FUN FACT

Coral reefs cover less than 1 percent of the ocean floor. But they are home to approximately 25 percent of all sea creatures.

Divers must be careful not to damage coral when they visit reefs.

shelter. People enjoy coral reefs as well. Divers love to swim near the corals. They admire these amazing animals and their beautiful colors and shapes.

FOCUS ON
CORAL REEFS

Write your answers on a separate piece of paper.

1. Write a letter to a friend that describes how coral reefs are formed.

2. Do you think people should be allowed to dive near coral reefs? Why or why not?

3. What kind of corals build reefs?

    A. soft corals

    B. stony corals

    C. all corals

4. How do coral reefs protect the coast?

    A. The waves splash against the coral reefs and water plants on shore.

    B. The waves wear away at the coral reefs instead of the shoreline.

    C. The waves go underneath the coral reefs and do not hit the shore.

5. What does **barrier** mean in this book?

*The reefs act like a **barrier**. Waves must go past the reefs to reach the shore.*

    A. a small part of something larger

    B. a fancy decoration used to make something more beautiful

    C. a structure placed in front of something to protect it

6. What does **delicate** mean in this book?

*In calmer areas, corals may be thinner or more **delicate**.*

    A. easily broken or damaged

    B. very hard and thick

    C. difficult to see

Answer key on page 32.

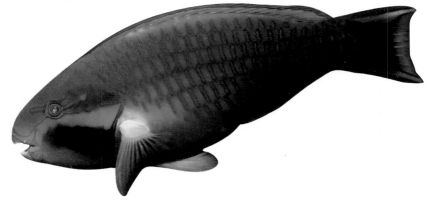

GLOSSARY

acidic
A chemical property that makes some things taste sour.

algae
Tiny, plant-like organisms that live in water and produce oxygen.

atoll
A ring of coral with a lagoon, or pool of water, inside it.

colonies
Groups of animals that live together and act as a single organism.

erosion
The act of wearing away a surface.

habitat
The type of place where plants or animals normally grow or live.

polyps
Ocean animals with tentacles and soft, tube-shaped bodies.

predators
Animals that hunt other animals for food.

reef
A ridge of rock, coral, or sand just below the ocean surface.

remains
Parts of a living thing that are left when it dies.

species
A group of animals or plants that are similar.

TO LEARN MORE

BOOKS

Fiedler, Heidi. *Coral: A Close-Up Photographic Look inside Your World.* Lake Forest, CA: Walter Foster Jr., 2017.

Gagne, Tammy. *Coral Reef Ecosystems.* Minneapolis: Abdo Publishing, 2016.

Ganeri, Anita. *Exploring Coral Reefs.* Chicago: Heinemann Library, 2014.

NOTE TO EDUCATORS

Visit **www.focusreaders.com** to find lesson plans, activities, links, and other resources related to this title.

INDEX

A
algae, 18–20, 24
atoll, 14

B
barrier reefs, 14

C
colonies, 6, 10
cup, 9–10

F
fish, 5, 25
food, 17–18, 26
fringing reefs, 14

G
Great Barrier Reef, 12

H
habitat, 12

I
island, 14

P
polyps, 6, 9–10, 17–19, 20–21, 24

S
seaweed, 23
shapes, 11, 14
shells, 6, 9–10, 17, 18, 21
shore, 14, 26
soft corals, 7
species, 7, 11
stony corals, 7

T
tentacles, 17

W
waves, 12, 26

Answer Key: 1. Answers will vary; **2.** Answers will vary; **3.** B; **4.** B; **5.** C; **6.** A